Level 2 is ideal for c
some reading instructi
simple sentences with

Special features:

subject words and concepts

Short, simple sentences

Let's celebrate Hanukkah

It's Hanukkah!

We light Hanukkah candles for eight nights.

Eight candles for eight nights!

We say prayers and sing.

16

17

Careful match between text and pictures

Happy Diwali!

We have a special Diwali dinner with our friends and family.

We have presents, too!

Happy Diwali!

Large, clear labels and captions

20

23

Educational Consultant: Geraldine Taylor

Book Banding Consultant: Kate Ruttle

LADYBIRD BOOKS

UK | USA | Canada | Ireland | Australia
India | New Zealand | South Africa

Ladybird Books is part of the Penguin Random House group of companies
whose addresses can be found at global.penguinrandomhouse.com.

www.penguin.co.uk www.puffin.co.uk www.ladybird.co.uk

Penguin
Random House
UK

First published 2017
004

Copyright © Ladybird Books Ltd, 2017

Printed in China

A CIP catalogue record for this book is available from the British Library

ISBN: 978–0–241–27523–8

All correspondence to
Ladybird Books
Penguin Random House Children's Books
One Embassy Gardens, 8 Viaduct Gardens, London SW11 7BW

Let's
Celebrate

Written by Ronne Randall
Illustrated by Becky Down

Contents

Let's celebrate

Here are some of the happy times we celebrate.

birthdays

Christmas

Hanukkah

Diwali

Eid

Happy birthday!

It's my birthday – my special day! Look at the birthday decorations.

Look at the birthday candles.
My friends and family sing
"Happy Birthday"!

We have special food and play games.

It's Christmas!

At Christmas time, we put on a special play at school. We sing and say prayers.

At home, we put up decorations and a Christmas tree, with lights. We put some presents by the tree.

Happy Christmas!

At Christmas time, we say "Happy Christmas" to our friends and family.

We have our presents by the tree, and I have Christmas dinner with my family.

15

Let's celebrate Hanukkah

It's Hanukkah!

We light Hanukkah candles for eight nights.

We say prayers and sing.

Happy Hanukkah!

Look! I have Hanukkah presents!

I play games with my friends.

We have special Hanukkah food, too.

Let's celebrate Diwali

It's Diwali! At Diwali, our home looks its best.

We put up our best decorations.

We sing and say prayers.

At night we light candles and special lights.

Happy Diwali!

We have a special Diwali dinner with our friends and family.

We have presents, too!

Let's Celebrate Eid

It's Eid! We look our best
to celebrate Eid.

We say prayers with our
family and friends.

Eid Mubarak!

We say "Eid Mubarak" to our friends and family.

We have a special dinner at Eid. We have presents at Eid, too!

Picture glossary

 candles

 decorations

 dinner

 family

 food

 friends

 games

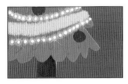 lights

 prayers

 presents

Index